EAST ANGLIAN STEAM
A PHOTOGRAPHIC TRIBUTE

Front Cover: KINGS LYNN 1948 *(G.A. Yeomans)*
Back Cover: NORWICH 1958 *(M. Fordham)*
Inside Front Cover: CROMER BEACH 1957 *(G.A. Yeomans)*
Inside Back Cover: MARKS TEY 1956 *(G.A. Yeomans)*
This Page: LIVERPOOL STREET 1959 *(K.J. Butcher)*
Centre Pages: NEAR SHENFIELD 1957 *(K.J. Butcher)*

Compiled by: **J.D. Mann**
Designed and published by: **South Anglia Productions**
26, Rainham Way, Frinton-on-Sea Essex CO13 9NS
Telephone: (01255) 677965
Copyright: **South Anglia Productions 1994**
Printed in Essex by: **Colourfast Ltd,** Colchester.
ISBN: 1 871277 23 X

Production of this album would not have been possible without the help of the following photographers: **K.J. Butcher, G.A. Yeomans, M. Fordham, P.J. Kelley, F. Hornby, L.R. Peters. P.J. Lynch, J.G. Dewing, E.R. Morten, D. Trevor-Rowe, J.A.C Kirke, F. Church.**

SHOREDITCH – May 13th 1958. Two J69's No' 68577/78 traverse the East London line with a Sunday excursion. **K.J. Butcher**

NEAR BENFLEET – November 4th 1961. Southend line steam action, Standard tank No. 80104 gets down to business on the L.T.S. route. **D. Trevor-Rowe**

BUSH HILL PARK – April 26th 1958. Another N7 No 69653 makes an impressive arrival on a bright spring morning. **K.J. Butcher**

RIPPLE LANE – November 31st 1959. Class 8F No 48492 departs from the yard with a substansial goods train. **F. Church**

NEAR SHENFIELD – April 24th 1949. A B12 under the wires, No 61571 passes on a Southend - Liverpool Street train prior to electrification. **J.G. Dewing**

COLCHESTER – May 24th 1958. The G.E. section was always short of motive power at busy weekends. B.R., class 4 No 76034 lends a hand on a down relief express. **F. Hornby**

COLCHESTER – September 7th 1957. K1's were reliable standby's for heavy passenger work. No 62053 sets out for Liverpool Street. **K.J. Butcher**

COLCHESTER – September 3rd 1957. An unusual but nevertheless effective angle on E4 No 62785, pictured between duties. **K.J. Butcher**

COLCHESTER – September 7th 1957. The up "East Anglian" passes with Britannia Pacific No 70034 "THOMAS HARDY" in charge. **K.J. Butcher**

GREAT BENTLEY – September 6th 1957. B1's No's 61363/61 pass with an ex-Clacton-on-Sea train. **K.J. Butcher.**

THORPE-LE-SOKEN – September 9th 1957. Essex Coast steam. A pre-electrification view of N7 No 69733 arriving from Walton-on-Naze with its customary three coaches. **K.J. Butcher**

IPSWICH – September 6th 1957. B12/3 No 61564 awaits departure with a train of mixed vehicles. **K.J. Butcher**

HAUGHLEY JUNCTION – July 5th 1952. A Laxfield train sets out for Mid-Suffolk headed by J15 No 65447. **L.R. Peters**

NORWICH (TROWSE) – September 5th 1952. East Anglian steam magnificence. 7MT No 70011 "HOTSPUR" with the up "NORFOLKMAN". **E.R. Morten**

WHITLINGHAM JUNCTION – August 15th 1959. Now preserved, N7 No 69621 passes the site of the long closed station with a Lowestoft-Norwich train. A light engine waits in the loop. **M. Fordham**

REEDHAM SWING BRIDGE – Summer 1960. Also preserved and now very much a celebrity engine, B12 No 61572 with the Lowestoft local goods. The scene is still the same today, but only "sprinters" venture to Lowestoft. **M. Fordham**

NORWICH (WENSUM JUNCTION) – June 14th 1958. A summer Saturday Yarmouth return working with B2 No 61617 "FORD CASTLE" in charge. **M. Fordham**

NORWICH (THORPE JUNCTION) – July 19th 1958. B17/6 No 61627 "ASKE HALL" and L1 No 67708 double head the 3.40pm Yarmouth to Norwich train. **M. Fordham**

NORWICH – May 22nd 1959. Memories of 32A. W.D. no 90191 runs onto the turntable. **M. Fordham**

NORWICH – June 28th 1959. East Anglian workhorse. J15 65469 simmers gently between duties. **M. Fordham**

NORTH WALSHAM (TOWN) – August 30th 1958. D16/3 No 62524 arrives with steam to spare. **K.J. Butcher**

SHERINGHAM – Summer 1957. Ivatt 4MT No 43147 runs in with the 4.22pm to Melton Constable in pre-preservation days. **G.A. Yeomans**

SUTTON BRIDGE – February 24th 1959. The 11.15am Spalding Town to Kings Lynn gets underway behind J6 No 64260. **P.J. Kelley**

SUTTON BRIDGE – February 24th 1959. Ivatt Class 4MT No 43107 on the 11.50am Kings Lynn to Peterborough North. The bridge survives today. **P.J. Kelley**

SUTTON BRIDGE – February 24th 1959. Another J6 No 64278 on an eastbound goods. (Class J freight, 10.58am Spalding Town to South Lynn.) **P J Kelley**

THETFORD – May 7th 1960.'01 No 63786 trundles through with a Whitemoor-Norwich pick up goods. **M Fordham**

NEAR FEN DITTON – August 2nd 1950. The East Anglian branch line scene of yesteryear. In early B.R. days E4 No 62781 heads for Mildenhall. **L.R. Peters**

CAMBRIDGE (CHESTERTON JUNCTION) – August 28th 1953. K1 No 62039 works a coal train from March via Ely. **L.R. Peters**

CAMBRIDGE – August 1961. J15 No 65457 arranges stock close to the end of steam at Cambridge. **J.A.C. Kirke**

CAMBRIDGE – 1956. Britannia No 70035 "RUDYARD KIPLING" leaves on an up Liverpool Street express and passes E4 No 62784. **L.R. Peters**

CAMBRIDGE – September 24th 1960. A view of the shed with K1 62039 in occupation. **J.A.C. Kirke**

CAMBRIDGE – April 20th 1953. Sister engines, B12/3's No 61569, with the tender from the rebuilt G.E.R. "Decapod"; pilots No 61561 on the 11.05am to Ipswich. **P.J. Lynch**

CAMBRIDGE – September 6th 1953. Immaculately turned out E4 No 62790 leaves with an R.C.T.S. special. **L.R. Peters**

AUDLEY END – August 26th 1953. B2 No 61617 "FORD CASTLE" with an up horse box special. **L.R. Peters**

AUDLEY END – August 26th 1953. Early in its G.E. career, Britannia No 70013 "OLIVER CROMWELL" speeds through the tunnel with an up Norwich - Liverpool Street (via Cambridge) train. **I R Peters**

HAVERHILL – September 9th 1957. J15 No 65470 arrives with the 11.38am Colchester to Cambridge train via the Stour Valley line. **K.J. Butcher**

CHAPPEL AND WAKES COLNE – September 9th 1957. A superb pre-preservation scene. J15 No 65442 arrives with the 12.01pm Marks Tey - Haverhill train via the Colne Valley line **K.L. Butcher**